Startled by
JOY

Gabriel's Horn Anthology of New Poetry

2019

Edited by Laura Vosika and Michael Dean

Startled by Joy

Edited and compiled by Laura Vosika and Michael Dean

Copyright 2019 Laura Vosika and Gabriel's Horn Press
All rights reserved.

No portion of this book may be reproduced, stored in any retrieval system, or transmitted in any form or by any means electronic, mechanical, photocopy, recording, scanning, or other except for brief quotations in reviews or articles, without the prior written permission of the author and publisher.

Cover photo: Eugene Mynzul
Cover design: Laura Vosika

Contact editors@gabrielshornpress.com
Published Minneapolis, Minnesota by Gabriel's Horn Press
First printing: May 2019 Printed in the United States.
ISBN-13: 978-1-938990-42-7
ISBN-10: ISBN-10: 1-938990-42-0

Table of Contents

What is Joy	5
Beauty	9
Moments	19
Humor	43
Hope	49
Bios	71
Afterward	83
Index	84

WHAT IS JOY

In the Faces

I found true joy in the little spaces -
Those overlooked by crowds of many
Joy - in the love in others' faces.

I visited many distant places -
Had audience with highest company,
I found true joy in the little spaces.

Children running in afternoon chases
From one another or a young nanny
Joy - in the love in others' faces.

On wilderness trails a flower graces
Ground between roots of a spreading oak tree -
I found true joy in the little spaces.

In the poorest of classes and races
They're still reaching out to be neighborly -
Joy - in the love in others' faces

Not in the wealthy and famous traces
was there anything of notice for me
I found joy in the little spaces.
Joy - in the love in others' faces.

– Deb Felio

Flows Out Like A Stream

I dreamt that I dwelt in marble halls
And hosted some elegant balls
Yet when Christmas came and then went
The halls had too pricey a rent.

To boast of a high ancestral name
And all of the Old South snobs to tame
Would mean I'd ignore DNA
Saying we're Clements, anyway.

I had riches too great to count
Would involve quite an act to mount
That I was the hope and the pride
Makes my brother fit to be tied.

Thought not a princess like Arline
I feel I know what Balfe does mean
For my mother loves me still the same
Which shows that she is quite a dame.

While I'm not "The Bohemian Girl"
With a noble knight who'll call me Pearl
I still relate to the maiden's dream

– Luisa Kay Reyes

Joy

When you sing soprano

And my hand is empty

And my heart is hollow

Your love is a royal flush

When I'm sick of playing Wild-cards,

I look at you

And I blush, portraying

A man once again in love

When you play the piano

The world goes into silent

Mode a hushed, concerto

That fills my soul with joy

– Mark Andrew Heathcote

BEAUTY

Summer Moon

Beneath the first full moon of summertime;
White foxglove opens, tips its bells to peek
Through wisps of fog and early sage... a sky,
A marigolden blossom in night's keep.

Behind the glow a spray of sparkling stars,
Is waiting for its turn to dazzle me;
Like lightning bugs in back-porch mason jars,
And hints of dawning ribbons rising east.

Across the tapestry dark's blushed orb flies;
Now wrapped in shining linen, flowing clouds,
Limned brilliantly in threads of gifted sighs,
Our human eyes awaiting dispersed shrouds.
A scintillating overlay remains;
Among the stars of summer, soft she wanes.

– Lorri Centineo

Dance in the Rain

Dancing in the rain

Sprinkles of silver falling

Glitter in my hair

– Annette Moore

Heliotropical

After a days bloom

All heads are turned west

For their evening kiss goodnight

And their floret crowns

Glow coppery pink

As the sun begins to sink

Into its own light.

– Donna Marie Beck

Swallowtails on the Sandbar

Here butterflies huddle, seven or eight
together, their wings folded up to show
difficult inscriptions—eyespots, ornate
glyphs that would tell us something angels know
if we could parse them. From the underside
I read them backwards, like old Adam perplexed
by the mystery of his unknown bride,
unnamed till he read her, then Death and Sex,
her scriptures in his body.
                                  The sand warms.
The air beats slowly with those mystic wings,
the mayflies rise and fall in dying swarms,
and from a hidden spot a brown wren sings.
She signals, *I am here! Now here! No, there!*
Hear me, love me, catch me, if you dare.

– J.S. Absher

Winter Beeches

When cold sun sifts down through the understory,

the beech leaves glow, like a brown-winged miller

that hovers round the street lamp and beats the powder

from its wings. This light is the modest glory

of our winter. On work days, when we speed

distracted here and there, we may not notice.

But walk near in the fog, half-past the solstice—

in February, when peepers start to breed:

the glow will draw us through the backlit haze

into an ashen spring. Now I think of this

half light in the August heat, as Joe-pye's

pink clouds smolder in the ditch and days

are growing shorter; as the lake's cool mist

clings to the pines and mutes the sun's slow rise.

– J.S. Absher

Publication credit: The Southern Poetry Anthology, VII: North Carolina (2014).

SAY SOMETHING

The wren has returned with her melodic scold.
Today I saw the first oriole, vivid
flame jacketed by black wings. From high
in a leafing cottonwood, a catbird let
loose its glossolalia.
                      The sky's a vibrant
solar blue. Lime-green and chartreuse leaves,
just opening, appear to dance unattached
in air, backlit by the early sun.
Birches dangle their brand-new catkins
like lures to catch our gaze.
                            It's hard to
know what to say about, what to say
to all this beauty to which we belong.
Saying nothing, our eyes praise by looking —
our ears, hearing, contribute to the song.

—Thomas R. Smith

Portrait

She smiles with ease, as lovely as a child;

And like a child she laughs with simple joys,

As though a candle's radiance were wild

Enough and life and love and men were toys.

Her girlish blush is coy and innocent,

Her slender form displays her elegance,

Her shoulder's curve is slim and delicate,

And all her movements sketch a feline grace.

Why does her beauty spark so much unrest?

How may her innocence exact such shame?

When she is near my loneliness has rest,

And love's seduction seems a harmless game.

But she contrives her lovely smile with ease,

And all her dear affections only tease.

— Tekkan

The Bridge

The bridge
Driving across
Seagulls gliding beside
Towards beauty, peace, belonging
Homeward

– Jacqueline Anderson

Rockport

Rockport
Jet skis, kayaks
Wade fishing Little Bay
Beach palapas casting cool shade
Inhale

– Jacqueline Anderson

Ebullient Bubbles

crickets chirp
beneath confetti clouds
Moet popping corks

my granddaughter laughs
an eighty-year-old man
called me kid

patio lanterns –
Van Gogh's starry night
right outside my door

morning blue sky
hoar frost glistens
light dances

elephant trumpeting
fills the air
morning light blazes
Here is the one
I have been waiting for

– Mary Vlooswyk

MOMENTS

Two Haiku on Family

1.

At Mother's Return
After long absence away
Children's Hearts So Thrilled

2.

Siblings in a group
Form alliances
Truly siblings love

– Marc T. Payne

My Boy

I saw my boy this morning, his face so full of joy,

He said,"Daddy, I'm a daddy now, and daddy, it's a boy!"

you don't have to worry dad, I know just what to do.

i'll raise my boy with lots of love ,the way you showed me to

he will know I love his mother, when he sees that every day.

Sowing seeds of family ties, you and mother showed the way.

when trouble comes to worry and he looks into my face

He will learn how adversity is handled here with grace.

We will all go fishing in that same Green Lake and stream,

if the big ones just aren't biting , we will all sit back and dream.

If he grows to be a sportsman, or an artist to the end,

He will know just as I do, that his daddy is his friend.

– Robert Henry Hoffman

Pinch Me Ghazal

Pinch me, doll, I can't believe it's real.

Is it what you think, or what you feel?

Am I wrong? Is it all just lies?

Or is romance really faith in disguise?

It's your heart I was meant to steal.

Don't think about it; go with what you feel.

Do we ever really know when it is real?

Sometimes you have to get right down and kneel.

That's right, we all believe in lies.

Romance is just faith in disguise.

Face it, Ed, you've lost sight of what is real.

Forget about what you think; it's what you feel.

– Ed Meek

MULLEIN, LATE JULY

Seedhead

so delicious

the downy woodpecker

pays no attention to us as

we pass.

– Thomas R. Smith

The Late Sonatas, Beethoven, Winter Sunday

On stage, a single

grand. Ten fingers robust as

an orchestra. Joy

turned over to us! Love made:

tears, fire, stars, their dissolving.

Program notes, Mark Mazullo: *I believe this music is (can be, and must be) about love, ultimately.*

– Suzanne Swanson

OAK LEAF

Oak leaf
twirling down through
the radiant air of
October, to you I whisper,
Well done.

– Thomas R. Smith

YOU KNOW HOW

after
a rain a wind
sweeps through the trees and makes
a second rain — memory is
like that

– Thomas R. Smith

Honeymoon

Side-by-side on a small white towel, we bask

In the sun smeared in coconut oil. I brush

Her cheek and she throws a smile. Then we

Go for a swim, take a walk, go shelling.

A master collector, her bucket fills

With angel wings and glassy moon shells.

Back at the towel, she sorts through her catch,

Picks out the perfect, tosses the rest.

Then we lean back, arms around our knees,

And watch the sun drop, and gulls circling,

And she tastes like salt and smells like limes

When she sits close, her head against mine.

Sweet Mary Murphy, beaming, bold,

She'll never leave me. We'll never grow old.

– Mary Beth Hines

written in the voice of my father

ON A BICYCLE

The speed, the turning pedals, the breeze
The sidewalk shade of maple trees
The roots that make the concrete
Swell, that make you stand up off the seat
Or swing out down a driveway to the street
A flash of sweater about the waist
And what is left
To show that I have passed –
A slash cut through a muddy mire
Or if the treads
Have just been through a puddle
Then the subtle
After-image of the tire,
A dog standing guard on a neighbor's lawn
Barking at something already gone
Or maybe a pile of leaves in the gutter
Settling with a breezy flutter
Stirred by a blast
Of something invisible, pedalling fast
And if I could make it last
A life I would
Phantom of the neighborhood

– Dan Blum

December Song

We slip from the forest on charmed, slender legs.

Our eyes spark with starlight, we dip our sleek heads

Toward the boy at the window reciting his prayers.

We're a dozen this evening – does, fawns, and a buck,

Streaming through twilight to lure the dear son

Of the camouflaged hunter, to daze him with musk,

To enchant him with emerald moss, ice, owl song,

Before he grows hungry, and skilled with a crossbow.

But the boy's still a baby, no need for our tricks.

He sees us in moonlight. We're gifts for a prince.

He steps out to greet us through snow cover, mist.

We kneel. He climbs on, nestles in for a ride,

While above Venus shines, and the Geminids fire.

– Mary Beth Hines

SIMMER

Late summer's simmer of cicada and
cricket counts the season, world's calendar.
Country ditches display modest bouquets
of Queen Anne's lace, chicory, red clover,
birdsfoot trefoil. A haze lies on bluish
potato fields, darkness between cornstalks
where a raccoon can safely dine and hide.
Some leaves have already curled up beside
the roads, the time of flourishing over,
the time of ripening to rot begun.
Sweat of noon creeps down the bicyclist's back.
Gardens splurge their bounty, earth giving life
its best possible chance. Clouds move in on
cool winds, shutting the sun out of the sky.

—Thomas R. Smith

Morning Coffee

First pink rays of dawn
Pouring over my garden
Brighten my coffee

– Annette Moore

Slippy Sun

A slippy sunny sunbeam
Slid right through my door
It dappled and danced
A happy dream
Upon my sad dirt floor
And suddenly sated
My gloom slid away
I remembered no more
Why I'd been so sad
That day

– Annette Moore

Troublemaker

I look forward to
the way we get lost at night.
Morning is too safe.

– Tony Plocido

My Stone Cat
A tanka

Fierce cat on my knee,
like a gargoyle, she protects
my lap from rivals.

She doesn't want my comfort,
only fealty (and fish).

– Sara Dovre Wudali

Sea Song

Rocky shore in a rocky land

Harp lifts its voice to gentle hand

Dances wind among the strings

Softly sighing, the soft breeze sings

Burbles the brook beside the song

It adds its voice and sings along

A child stops to listen and see

Pirouettes with joy and glee

Her skirt spins out and her hair blows free

Waving her arms and clapping her hands

On a rocky shore in a rocky land

– J.A. Sellers

come remember

come with me remember
the spring before the fall
come with me my love
can you still recall

a sparsely furnished flat
casement opened wide
sitting silently
as wind and leaf confide

scene of setting sun
blushing against sky
robed in redolence
of the day gone by

penning poems of pleasure
upon lover's back
as starlight's flickered flames
burned from altar black

time was ours alone
just wed bride and groom
as we emerged each morn
from blankets of cocoon

beauty blessing born
billowed on new wings
hovered upon heights
in search of songs to sing

now we stop to rest
upon highest branch
unique vantage point
above circumstance

see river of time
purling in the sun
rise and fall of earth
change as plans undone

squinting barely see
the promise of a plan
tale of tapestry
obscured from every man

on anniversary
let us resolve to rest
and with the past proclaim
that we are richly blessed

– Carter Norman

On Making Snow Angels with My Son

What print of what mad spirit sparkles there

And mars the fluid white with impish stain?

Its wings have vanished into gelid air,

But frantic flap-marks tellingly remain.

A seal, a stamp, formed not in molten wax

But in the frigid fire of winter's charm,

Leaves traces of such violent attacks

That one still hears the echoing alarm.

It tinkles from each naked, trembling twig

But harks of laughing mother and her son—

An ancient root that sprouts a modern sprig.

(Insects in amber with today's are one.)

Oh, let such joys—attempted, won, and prized—

Be in my heart forever fossilized.

– Rebecca Hope

Ride, Charlie

With a newspaper rolled in my pocket

and a grocery bag of whisky and cheese

I ride my bike to wherever I please -

to family, to friends, to the road again.

My spinning wheels are alight

there is freedom at every turn,

the routes all lead to the same bright end

and all of the signs read home.

(for my dad)

– Donna Marie Beck

echoes of the morn

sighing with the setting sun
we watched then hand in hand
as an orb of opulence
slipped beneath the land

lake burned brightly for a time
played upon your eyes
how they danced in dying light
as twin fireflies

stars danced petite pirouettes
in ballroom of the night
every blink bore back to us
coquettish candlelight

suns seamed into diamonds
bright and bejeweled gown
worn by our romance
royal newly crowned

I see you there so soft and kind
as echoes of the morn
who are the children of the sun
his special sweet first born

when shawls of grace cast down on us
kept us from the cold
and everything we dearly loved
could not be bought nor sold

as children then we walked the trails
of gilt and shadowed strands

for all the world was erudite
and magic ruled the land

so sweet your simple smile
a maiden in the spring
so dear your sojourn eyes
that gave my writing wings

made each poem a bird on branch
which fluttered toward the sun
filled the sky with sweet soft song
until the day was done

then in heart they'd nest at night
sleep beneath the stars
nestled in the after light
of suns which sojourn far

I wear this robe in wintertime
when drafts slip across floor
whenever ardent appetite
longs for something more

whenever sedate sentiments
stirred aren't strong enough
whenever mantle above hearth
requires a dust

there I store sweet memories
the ones I set apart
as mind displays its sentiments
above a flaming heart

– Carter Norman

On Kianna Turning Two

When Kianna has a party

She invites her teddy bears

To take her guest's attendance

From their posts upon the stairs

When Kianna has a party

She wears her brother's shirt

And tucks it round her middle

For a flouncy hula skirt

When Kianna has a party

She hangs banners and balloons

With paper golden dragons

Under paper silver moons

When Kianna has a party

She borrows Mommy's pearls

And powder for her rosy cheeks

Just like a grownup girl

When Kianna has a party

She dances and she sings

She opens all the presents

And gets tangled in the strings

When Kianna has a party

She dons her Daddy's cap

She laughs and then she giggles

As she's dandled on his lap

When Kianna has a party

She has ice cream on her cake

And blows out a festive candle

For every wish she'll make

When Kianna has a party

She plays with her new toys

Like electronic Elmo

That makes such silly noise

When Kianna has a party

She says goodnight with a kiss

To friends and family gathered

Who wave "Farewell, Little Miss"

– Chris Reid

ode to yeats

I rose from bed habit bred

on lilt of latent light

for solace sought beyond plot

of tired troubled life

to contemplate sojourn fate

with poor philosophy

while sky gave birth in radiant mirth

from fertile womb of sea

stepped to an unguarded edge

and felt mortality

was but a vapor upon sky

amidst eternity

wafting came a redolence

stoked by fragrant fire

that made me close coat against cold

and turn toward my desire

reformed was I by solitude
by ceaseless waves of wind
so joyful sought familiar brood
as one reprieved of sin

I coursed across the ancient bog
beyond the meadow's veil
where the light falls fresh and bright
as milk into a pail

came upon a cottage fair
whose roof was thatched with wheat
rising from its hidden hearth
was fragrance strong and sweet

but sweeter yet beyond the latch
with soft insistent care
was the one I dearly loved
patiently waiting there

– Carter Norman

all we knew

I awake to our brief dawn
returning as favorite song
golden sentiment of sun
chestnut hair come all undone
fragrance born upon soft breeze
hinting at each honey bee
there we sat late afternoons
blushing under evening sky
lights turned low bore silhouettes
upon irises of eyes
covers curled about your back
breath faded and then came back
corner curled around your dress
covetous as my caress
scattered garments upon floor
fabric of our favored lore
morning mused with mellow mind
took away as turpentine
incremental evening ink
diluted in sun's bright sink
inside small flat on avenue
when you and I were all we knew

– Carter Norman

HUMOR

WRITING A SONNET

How do you make a sonnet? You gather

words and propel yourself into a rhyme

you can't foresee, scrapping words you'd rather

use for those that can more readily climb

the kind of wall you've agreed to. And the odd

thing is how the words begin to form

the thought, your ear pitches forward like a god

determined to catch a certain country in his storm.

And so far, so good, until the end

which abruptly breaks from your plan

and leads you at least halfway around the bend

into chaos, and all your efforts then

must be to muster poetic muscle, start

to turn the thing around and find a way out.

—Thomas R. Smith

POEM OF PLIGHT

For you my only love, my dear
Tonight an unabashed leer
For the shorts that top your thigh
A bold and surreptitious eye
As of someone calmly nosing
By the local bank at closing
Probing, trying to decide
The best way he may slip inside

For my beloved one a leer
Upon her soft and blanching rear
A gaze upon the after-trail
Of her pirouetting tail
Then a glance into her eyes
As she looks back to realize
The tingling in her derriere
Is just a warming to my stare

And in our eyes as they unite
An overture, a plea, a plight
The silent stirrings of dispute
The suitor and the counter suit
And all the gestures that comprise
The promise of her compromise

This is all I bring tonight
A leer, a poem, a manly plight
A hope, a brazen look, a plea
Dear one, it is up to thee

– Dan Blum

Confessions of a Non-Foodie

(An Alphabet Poem)
Anyone can cook, says Chef Gusteau,
But I recoil and scream, "Oh, no!"
Culinary exploits excite my friends,
Dietary devotees who delight in new trends.
Everyone raves about food except me.

Foodies post goodies to my Facebook wall,
Grocery lists, recipes, menus, and all.
Huevos rancheros appear in the morning;
In the evening prosciutto pops up without warning.
(Just chips and cheese fill me, not figs and brie.)

Kale has more uses than salt now, it seems.
Lamb L'Arabique sends you off to sweet dreams.
Mousseline for dessert could please a dictator.
Nouvelle or haute cuisine sooner or later
Overwhelm me with multi-hued majesty.

Prawns Provencale or Shrimp Embrochette,
Quiche Florentine with Eggplant Croquette.
Ragout or rag-out: I can't even pronounce
Some of the things they dispense by the ounce
To make those grandiose dishes I see.

Uninspired by feats of gustatory splendor,
VitaMix at hand, I fix my shake in the blender.
While others eat gourmet, I'm almost but not quite
Xylophagous—which gives me more time to write.
You won't understand if you're one of those food nerds:
Zest, spice, and flavor—for me—come from words.

– Rebecca Hope

He Gets the Credit

(a double dactyl poem)

Hippety Hoppety
President Jefferson
Loved to accumulate,
Found it a lark,

Having no credit cards
(Pre-shopaholically),
Charged his new purchase
To Lewis and Clark.

(As the third president of the United States, Thomas Jefferson acquired the Louisiana Purchase, which he commissioned Lewis and Clark to explore.)

– Rebecca Hope

A Few Eights on my Plate

Eight eyes like lemurs' open-wide stare
(Eight chuckles giggling under my breath)
Eight tanned mucky legs from thighs to toes
And eight grimy paws reaching forward to show
Gelatinous findings and wriggling masses
A buzz and some flickers in smudged jelly glasses
Wiggly creatures, eight buckets of weeds
Eight nature offerings, four silent pleas-

PLEASE, oh PLEASE may we just keep these?

Just how many frog eggs in one grimy paw?
Were those salt or freshwater crabs that I saw?
I counted to ten, hoped to find calm reserve
How much of this offering do I deserve?

Life greets me in often uncountable blessings
Sometimes, though, the counting is part of the lesson.

– Lorri Centineo

HOPE

New Joy

Come to the water, come to the spring
Drink of refreshing and cool blue water
Rest in the shade where the linky birds sing
And the river's alive with the laugh of the otter

Step far away from the bonds of the night
Throw off its chains of jealous and malice
The dreams of the dark shrink far from the light
The wine of new joy will fill your gold chalice

– J.A. Sellers

Still the Birds Sang

The night was dark and still the birds sang
Their voices sparkled in the trees and rang
Across the shadowed, murky land
Telling poor souls, *The light is at hand!*

The day dawned slow and the birds sang out
A trill and a lilt and a great joyous shout
As the sun burst out and flooded the land
Telling pour souls, *The light is at hand!*

– J.A. Sellers

Dance

The island waits for spring's delayed return
And I on mainland stand and wait as well,
This lake is slow to give in to God's call
To melt, release its frozen depths and dance
With shards aglitter, sparkling, beckoning home
Those wanderers strayed, unseen for months before.

Today the darkness slowly lifts before
The island pines reveal in sun's return
An aerie awaiting the eagles coming home;
Across the strait my family waits as well
While sun ignites these woods and shadows dance
Along the shore, a moose begins to call.

The day unfolds and soon another call
Then silence like a pause before
The music starts and all begin to dance,
A call to a dance inviting me to return
To live again a way once known well,
A way renewed each day when I am home.

Family love beckons home
Listening I hear the clear call,
Inviting me to live here well.
Dear ones who came before
Await with open arms my safe return
To take my place in their love's dance.

On dappled shore the daisies dance,
This is their true and natural home,
Their white crowns mark the late spring's slow return,
When dusk descends loons begin their piercing call
From hidden nests for they learned long before
That young life here must be guarded well.

A lesson from the wild to be learned well,
I must begin again to live this dance,
For the one that I had tried before
Would not bring me home;
To live in simplicity and gratitude is my true call
God's grace notes bid a safe return.

To live well, to be at home,
To learn my dance, that is the call
That opens my heart to joy's return.

– J M Bollman

Propitiation

Accused, I stand alone before the judge,

Trembling as I hear the lawyer scoff

To list my crimes: the filth, the muck, the sludge,

Right down to hidden stains I can't wipe off.

How can I plead? I'm guilty of each charge.

I am undone! The accusing counsel sneers

At my distress, my obvious guilt writ large

Upon my face. Surrounded by the jeers

Of the disgusted crowd I hide my head.

Worse than the guilt is its attendant Shame,

Which strips me bare. But what is this? Instead

Of bearing scorn, I scoff myself. My blame

Rests on his naked shoulders! --
                                My judge, who
Himself hangs on my gallows, breathes, "For you."

– Kim Schneider

August Morning

The run of rain from the tops of eaves

falls on the herbs and the phlox,

gathers in droplets upon the green,

refreshes the glad in the flower box.

Late summer thunder rumbles the air,

 behind the pour and the gush,

and all the hosannas are laid bare

before cessation, a holy hush.

The landscape, it listens,

the leaves fold in prayer

around drops that glisten,

bejeweling sanctified air.

Laughing and lightsome, the joy of the storm,

blessing the plants and awaiting corm.

– Donna Isaac

My Now Departed Brother

So, "Oh, happy fall!" some people say,
    explaining away
        all confusion of God's plan,
        thinking man
            was destined to fall
                through God's active intention
                    for our behavior.

Thank God,
    that through the envy of the devil
        death entered the world,
        so Jesus Christ
            could become our Savior.

However, God always intended
    us to live lives that never ended
        in the Eden of Earth.

No, the sadness and pain
    of our fall
        actually came
            from selfish choices,
            but selfless revision
            ends our division,
            so we can rejoice.

'Tis impossible that He never intended
               to send Himself—
               through His Spoken Word—
               and yes, thank God
                     for death!

After all,
       after our happy fall,
       we can return to unity
       with our Father,
       through His Son,
       in their Spirit.

But there is no reason to believe
       He did not in fact conceive
       a divine plan
             to speak Himself
                   into the incarnation
                     of man,
                         loving us so much
                           that through His physical touch,
                               even without our fall
                         we would see
                             we are incarnate
souls,
                           not each a soul
                           trapped inside a body.

Oh, God bless you,
    my now departed brother,
        best friend of all those years,
        dead now from a motorcycle crash
        and cause of all my tears!

You are gone from me—
    and Mom and Dad and family—
    but through all of our prayers
    and trust in Jesus' Divine Mercy,
        through the grace of God
        we can be
            a communion of saints
                sharing in the beauty
                of all our prayers for each other,
                you remembering me
                and me remembering you,
            my brother in mutual memory of brother,
            always connected
                to each other.

– Mark Connor

Making Do

In the clover fields, the bees alight

on bushy flowers, purple and white.

Soft rabbits chew the tender leaves

close by a fence where a spider weaves

pearly wreaths, like a tiny wheelwright.

This is the prairie in the day, bright

and shining like a sea of light,

waves of grasses, wafting sheaves

in the clover fields.

To many, the prairie is home, a delight,

a soughing field, a welcome sight.

But I miss a mountain, and my heart grieves

a lost horizon and makes believe

I see a blue ridge in pale twilight

beyond the clover fields.

– Donna Isaac

Upon the Finishing of my House Fried Rice

Upon the finishing of my House Fried Rice from
    Kim's Chinese restaurant
        while sitting on the bench by the tennis courts
            overlooking
            the baseball fields
                on Prior Avenue,
        enjoying the afternoon sun
            on my chest and legs,
            the Author of wisdom
            reached me
                through a fortune cookie.

"You have a yearning for perfection."

'Tis a sharp observation,
    accurate and true;
    parentally harsh
        and merciful, too.
    Inwardly searching
        I easily see
        my old defection to an Empire of fear,
        one that ruled me
        in a spiral of failure
        till my childlike trust
        helped lead me here.

My yearning for perfection
        I still hold dear.

    Yet with the press of this pen
            onto paper again
            I gratefully accept failure.
After all, only the taking of
              another step
gets me almost there,
                  saving me from nowhere.
    Only humility protects me while here,
        defeating my arrogance.

So with the press of this pen
        I try once again
        to end my poem here,
            knowing I know,
            however I know,
      we—
                children born in the Kingdom of Love—
                humbly outlive the empire of fear.

– Mark Connor

Softer Rain

This heart's a fountainhead outpouring joy!
 For knowing you are here by me each night,
The cold outside another world away,
What cannot touch this heat nor burning bright.

You tell me no cool river flows around,
Nor softens souls, once hardened by deceit,
For even yours might lock itself away?
Denying human need; admit defeat?

Perhaps a softer rain will fall, will touch,
As healing salts of tears on tired cheeks;
A face uplifted to my gentle show'r
Will find pure, fresh-kissed love your longing seeks.

No spring forever flows on driest slopes,
But waterdrops feed flow'rs with nascent hopes.

– Lorri Centineo

Mystic Rose

I gaze with joy at every hour

Upon a secret mystic flower,

A luminous rose burning bright

Shining with everlasting light.

The jeweled rose petals enfold

Within my heart a throne of gold,

Upon that throne a diamond star,

More dazzling yet than those afar –

Trembles with a steady glow,

Its flame to leap, its light to grow,

Day by day with great endeavor,

Breaks bonds like a flooded river,

Till one day, like the sun above,

I'll be a blazing torch of love.

– Lilly Gellé

Untitled

Replace in your eyes the profound sadness

With gay dancing lights radiating joy,

Make those rare diamonds shine with happiness,

Remove from your life all things which annoy,

Pile at your feet the treasures I amass,

Place by bare soul there, your new shining toy,

My heart, full of song, prayer and caress,

A fortress of love nothing can destroy-

Build a golden bridge to Heaven – no less—

Is the sweetest task I would most enjoy.

– Lilly Gellé

The Transformer

He is the laughter of God

Still calling us

To leave our nets,

To take the risk

Of radical love.

And those who will be poured out,

He still turns to wine.

– Teresa Burleson

Joy Jumps Heart To Heart

From heart to heart
like a grasshopper.
But all I need do is but hover
over zenith green-tips of dew.

All I need do' is but dance
above His skies grey purlieu
to feel His rainbows lance
and not feel blue.

All I need do' is but touch wings
with His mirror-ball awnings
His unworldly, light!
'Then learn heaven is truly-bright.

All I need learn is to be still…
Like a grasshopper
He can but net at will
Clasp in His palms prayer
Our sinful souls free of sin forever.

– Mark Andrew Heathcote

I should like

Pray, tell your vision of the afterlife?

Is there a seed invested, still to grow?

Who'll germinate it in the next afterlife?

I should, like to see it leave its embryo,

I should like to water it daily, between

Dusk and dawn; watch its vines twist and climb,

I'd like to see a sapling tree, waving green

Her boughs bent following the moon, downstream.

I should like your roots knitted deeply in me

A hopeless romantic sings eternal joy,

Yet-knows the limitations of their plea

I'd like to be there, when your eyes, reemploy

Open like dew-wet flowers ever so coy,

A Helen that's beautiful as that of Troy.

– Mark Andrew Heathcote

sweet virgin of the sacred door

oh virgin bride whose love surpassed

whose holy yes came to pass

in humble start as you knelt down

to bear the thorns of servant's crown

intercede dear blessed one

call upon your sacred son

for he cannot deny your voice

he in love has lost all choice

sweet celestial virgin queen

make for me an offering

upon altar of your love

offer it to son above

he will never turn away

the dawn of his brief earthly day

who held him close and rocked him mild

whose soft sweet songs he heard as child

I would be as babe you bore

call you mother evermore

rocked as your sweet infant son

until night on earth is done.

till' I awake to heavens dawn

rising in salvation's song

until then come hold my hand

I am child understand

whose body can't reflect his soul

I am old yet nothing know

teach me of humility

studied in your sacristy

oh radiant rose whose righteous bloom

never fades above the tomb

weave for me a sacred shawl

wrap this child weak and small

your blessed beauty I adore

sweet virgin of the sacred door

– Carter Norman

Golden Bumble Bees

My bulbous head is a beehive humming
With thoughts and one by one the bees go forth
Voracious for sugary nectar and
Rumbling bumbling and bobbing in summer

But a single bee doesn't amount to
Much it's cumulative exploration
It's a happenstance discovery of
A juicy flower informing the hive

Where the sweetness is and directing the
Buzzing swarm to the garden that hundreds
Of little bee feet may trod on silky
Petals that a multitude of tiny

Bee straws may altogether burrow in
And with accumulating effort suck.

I may be thoughtful
assuming a studious
expression sporting
a furrowed brow but really
I want my juicy honey.

– Tekkan

(This is a sonnet without rhyme and a Japanese Tanka.)

BIOS

FEATURED POETS

Thomas R. Smith

Thomas R. Smith has had hundreds of poems published on three continents. His poems and essays have appeared in numerous journals and anthologies and in *Editor's Choice II* (The Spirit That Moves Us Press) and *The Best American Poetry 1999* (Scribner). His work has reached national audiences on Garrison Keillor's Writer's Almanac and in former US Poet Laureate Ted Kooser's syndicated newspaper column, American Life in Poetry.

He is author of eight books of poems, *Keeping the Star, Horse of Earth, The Dark Indigo Current, Winter Hours, Waking Before Dawn, The Foot of the Rainbow, The Glory,* and *Windy Day at Kabekona: New and Selected Prose Poems*. A chapbook of nature poems, *Kinnickinnic*, appeared in 2008 from Parallel Press. He has edited Airmail: The Letters of Robert Bly and Tomas Tranströmer (Graywolf Press, 2013)*Walking Swiftly: Writings and Images on the Occasion of Robert Bly's 65th Birthday* (Ally Press, 1992; HarperCollins, 1993) and *What Happened When He Went to the Store for Bread* (Nineties Press, 1993), a selection of the best of the Canadian poet Alden Nowlan, now in its second edition.

His poetry criticism has appeared in the St. Paul Pioneer Press, the Minneapolis Star Tribune, Great River Review, Ruminator Review, and other periodicals. He is a Loft Foreword Program poetry instructor at the Loft Literary Center in Minneapolis. He and his wife, the artist Krista Spieler, live in River Falls, Wisconsin.

Robert Bly writes: "Thomas R. Smith is a high-spirited poetry horse riding over the hills of emotion."

Dan Blum

Dan Blum's most recent book is *The Feet Say Run* (Gabriel's Horn Press, 2016), a literary novel set in World War II. The novel tells the tale of Hans Jaeger in Nazi Germany, the Jewish girl he loved, and his years fighting with the Wehrmacht.

Blum is also the author of *Lisa 33* (Viking Press, 2003), the influential postmodern comedy set on the Internet, which was published under the pseudonym *Dan Allan* and received positive attention and reviews from *Kirkus Reviews* and *Entertainment Weekly*.

Blum was interviewed by *Psychology Today* on the challenges of writing and publishing fiction. He has appeared on the popular Spectrum Books podcast speaking about the transition from a publishing deal with a New York publishing house to working with an independent publisher.

Blum has also spoken extensively with the literary community about the writing process and ethics of his content.

Blum runs a humor and political satire blog *The Rotting Post*, which is co-branded as *The Trumplandia Review*.

ALL POETS

J.S. Absher

J.S. Absher's first full-length book, *Mouth Work*, won the 2015 Lena Shull Book Competition sponsored by the NC Poetry Society and was published by St. Andrews University Press. Previous chapbooks are *Night Weather* (Cynosura Press, 2010) and *The Burial of Anyce Shepherd* (Main Street Rag, 2006). His work has been published in approximately 45 journals and anthologies, including *Visions International, NC Literary Review, Tar River Poetry,* and *Southern Poetry Anthology, VII: North Carolina.* In 2019 He won the Clint Larson Poetry Prize from *BYU Studies Quarterly.* He lives with his wife, Patti, in Raleigh, NC.

Jacqueline Anderson

Jacqueline Anderson currently lives in the city Rockport on the Texas coast. She is a member of the Aransas County Poetry Society. Her writing style is upbeat and affirmative. Jacqueline enjoys Texas travel, kayaking and the beautiful beaches of south Texas. Find Jacqueline at
https://www.facebook.com/aransascountypoets
https://www.facebook.com/poemsonthegoac/

Donna Marie Beck

Donna is an English mum of two who has been practicing poetry since her 20's. She has appeared in anthologies, the first one being *Soul Feathers.* She is now writing a story about a young woman in search of the sun. Donna says, "If I didn't write half of me would be hidden inside."

J.M. Bollman

J M Bollman, also known as Jana Preble, found joy in her childhood reading poetry and writing rhyming vignettes of daily activities. However, in the schools she attended, the writing emphasis was on research reports and journalism. She found the same to be true in her undergraduate and graduate school studies. After years of university graduate school teaching, Jana has come home again to writing and thanks to the encouragement of her husband, poet Charles Preble, she has returned to the joy of her childhood, writing poetry.

Teresa Burleson

Teresa Burleson has been free-lancing for over 35 years and has credits in over 45 magazines. In 2002, she received the National League of American Pen Women Virginia Liebeler Biennial Grant for Mature Women in the letters category. She published The Pilgrim's Lyre in 2003 and A Rose Without Thorns in 2013. For her, writing is a calling. She makes her home in Central Texas with her wonderful husband and red dog named Fiona.

Lorri Centineo

Lorri lives on the coast of Maine where she pursues interests in math, science, music, and art. To lighten her less-than-lyrical load of technical writing, she combines science with literature in a STEM environment and for fifteen years has taught mythology of the night sky in a planetarium. Encouraging her students to use the starry backdrop as a venue for poetry reignited her own joy of poetry and verse. She has written, illustrated and published three poetic children's books that she claims are really for grandparents, and two books of poetry.

Mark Connor

Mark Connor is from St. Paul, MN. A boxer since age 10, he currently trains competitive and recreational boxers, runs a training business called *Fighting Chance/Boxing for Life* and writes fiction, poetry, and journalism. He has written and published many articles about Boxing and Irish culture and history, as well as other features. This is his first creative publication. The poem *My Now Departed Brother* was written for David James Ruiz, March 7, 1969—September 26, 2019, a friend since 3rd grade who died in a motorcycle crash. www.boxersandwritersmagazine.com

Deb Felio

deb y felio is a witness poet exploring and writing on the mundane, the miraculous and the under-represented sides of historic and current issues. She lives and writes in the hills of Boulder, Colorado and is active in the Denver Lighthouse for Writers and the Stain'd Art community. Her work is published in multiple online venues including *Writing In a Woman's Voice, Tuck* magazine, The Poet by Day, Right Hand Pointing, Quatrain.fish and *With Painted Words*. In print are anthologies *Hay(na)ku* (Eileen Tabios, editor) and in *Minnie's Diary, A Southern Literary Review* October 2018.

Lilly Gellé

Lilly Gellé was born in Hungary in 1907. She came to the United States at age 16 for an arranged marriage. Lilly was a trained pianist but when she moved to California in her later years, she also started writing poetry, publishing it with her local church.
Lilly's poems were submitted by her granddaughter, Laurie Kehoe, an author.

Mark Andrew Heathcote

Mark Andrew Heathcote is from Manchester in the UK, author of "In Perpetuity" and "Back on Earth" two books of poems published by a CTU publishing group ~ Creative Talents Unleashed and in creative charge, direction of two anthologies by the same publisher. He is an adult learning difficulties support worker, who began writing poetry at an early age at school. Mark enjoys spending his leisure time off work reading and writing and spending time gardening.

Mary Beth Hines

A recently retired project manager, Mary Beth Hines studied literature and creative writing at The College of the Holy Cross. She is an active participant in Boston area writing workshops. Her work has been published, or is forthcoming, in journals such as the Aurorean, Blue Unicorn, Crab Orchard Review, The Road Not Taken, and Brilliant Flash Fiction. When she's not reading or writing, she's swimming or happily playing with her new grandson – an inspiration for much of her recent writing.

Robert Henry Hoffman

Bob Hoffman, born in Albert Lea, MN, has worked as an ocean sonographer, forest fire fighter, and teacher. He has published a book of poetry and short-stories titled, "Paperboy Memories" Of his writing, he says: "I write most every day and do copper sculptures. My poetry comes from unexpected experiences, and from my coffee buddies and the stories they tell. Majority of what I write rhymes, because of the joy I find in rhymes." Bob, with his wife of 51 years, has four children and seven grand children.

Rebecca Hope

Rebecca May Hope delights in reading and writing the well-crafted phrase. While wordsmithing is its own reward, her weekly writers' group provides the impetus to keep writing and polishing. Rebecca couldn't imagine a life without teaching; her middle school, high school, and college students give her a chance to

share her passion for words with a new crop of young people each year. When she's not teaching or writing, you'll find Rebecca playing with or rocking her grandbabies, walking her rambunctious ninety-pound Labradoodle on wooded nature trails, or pampering her softer-than-air Ragdoll cat.
www.RebeccaMayHope.com

Donna Isaac

Poet Donna Isaac is a teaching artist who helps organize community readings in the Twin Cities through Cracked Walnut and Blue Harbor Center for the Arts. Published work includes a poetry book, *Footfalls* (Pocahontas Press), a paean to American folk music and her formative years growing up in the Appalachians; two chapbooks, *Tommy* (Red Dragonfly Press); *Holy Comforter* (Red Bird Chapbooks); and work in journals, e.g., *Pine Mountain Sand & Gravel, The Penn Review, The Saint Paul Almanac*. A new chapbook, *Persistence of Vision*, is forthcoming from Finishing Line Press in fall 2019. donnaisaacpoet.com

Ed Meek

Ed Meek writes poetry, fiction, articles and book reviews. His most recent books are *Spy Pond*, poems, and *Luck*, short stories. He has been published in WBUR's *Cognoscenti, The Sun, The Paris Review,* and *The Boston Review.* Follow him on Twitter @emeek. His website is edmeek.net

Annette Moore

Annette is a native of Virginia currently living in New England where she loves to garden and visit the ocean, both of which are favorite subjects of her writing. After many years in business, she began writing poetry in 2016. She loves poetry for its ability to speak great truths and wisdom succinctly and in unique ways.

Carter Norman

Carter Norman has spent over 25 years in Education, teaching regular and special education and at elementary, secondary and post secondary levels. His poetry has won awards from The League of Minnesota Poets, The Missouri State Poetry Society and The Minnesota Library Association. He has been published in Inscape, Willows Wept Review and the St. Paul Almanac. He is the author of two books, *Fields of Flowers* and *Dancing with the Wind* (self published).

Marc T. Payne

Marc is originally from Virginia, (the state, not the city in Minnesota) but now, consequently, lives in Minnesota, with his family. He finds inspiration through his faith in God, family, animals, nature and human interaction. He started writing poetry in middle and high school. Many things inspire writing, for him: love, joy, God's attributes, pain, happiness, sadness, nature, beauty, and more. Already intrigued by creativity, in other ways (drawing, pottery, painting), writing was, yet, another place to extend his heartfelt drive to write. Encouragement, excitement and humility, he feels, being included in this work.
Find Mark @MrIndigo91 at Twitter

Tony Plocido

Tony Plocido started writing poetry in high school. Since then he has published three books. His latest, *Felt This so Many Times*, released September 2019. Currently he is the Host/Curator for the Poets & Pints Reading Series and a Board member of Cracked Walnut.

Chris Reid

Chris Reid is a long time Chicago slam poet and past winner of the Contemporary American Poetry Prize. Her work has appeared

in *Journal of Modern Poetry, Midwest Review, Rhino, Saudade, World Order* and other journals. Chris teaches ESL and is a student of Arabic language at the University of Chicago. She is raising two fabulous children in the outer suburbs.
Look for her spoken word performance on YouTube at Waterline Writers.

Luisa Kay Reyes

Luisa Kay Reyes' work has been featured in *The Raven Chronicles, The Windmill, The Foliate Oak,* and other literary magazines. Her essay, "Thank You", is the winner of the April 2017 memoir contest of The Dead Mule School Of Southern Literature. Her Christmas poem was a first place winner in the 16th Annual Stark County District Library Poetry Contest. Her essay "My Border Crossing" received a Pushcart Prize nomination from the Port Yonder Press. Two of her essays were nominated for the *Best of the Net* anthology and another was featured on "The Dirty Spoon" radio hour.
https://www.facebook.com/LuisaKayReyesWriter/

J. A. Sellers

After growing up on a farm in Nebraska, J.A. Sellers earned degrees in philosophy and English, which led, through unexpected twists and turns, to a career in finance and banking, which led to the opportunity to travel, particularly to Eastern Europe and Asian, to study many cultures, and return finally to writing and poetry. J.A. is currently working on a first book of poetry.

Kim Schneider

Kim Schneider is a German teacher, wife, and adoptive mother who has always been in love with language—both its creative, expressive possibilities as well as its structure. She writes in a variety of genres, including poetry, memoir, and plays, the latter primarily for church performances. One of her memoirs won the

Obsequious Beanpod Award for prose in her college literary magazine and several poems in German earned scholarship awards. As an educator, Kim enjoys sharing her love of language and culture with younger generations and guiding them to be world citizens.

Suzanne Swanson

Suzanne Swanson is the author of *House of Music* and the chapbook *What Other Worlds: Postpartum Poems*. She is a winner of the Loft Mentor Series and was one of the founders of Laurel Poetry Collective. Her poems have appeared in literary journals and in the Land Stewardship Letter. Suzanne rows on the Mississippi River and is happiest near big water.

Tekkan

Tekkan is the Dharma name for Barry MacDonald. He has lived in England, Japan, and Minnesota, all of which have influenced him. The themes of his life revolve around his Buddhist practice and his recovery from addiction. His books, "Everyday Mind," look for the extraordinary hidden within everyday events. He uses the sonnet form without the rhyme scheme followed by a Japanese tanka.

Mary Vlooswyk

Mary is an emerging poet from Calgary, Alberta. In March 2018 her poetry was shortlisted for Quattro Books inaugural Best New Poet In Canada contest. She placed third in a Canada 150 Poetry Contest. Her writing has appeared in Haiku Canada anthologies, *Asahi Shimbun, Mother's Always Write, FreeFall, GUSTS, MoonBathing, Gift of Silence: an anthology tribute to Leonard Cohen, Never Ending Story* anthology, and most recently *The Wild Musette*. Mary loves and is inspired by the outdoors. She is a student of cello but has an eclectic playlist.

Sara Dovre Wudali

Sara Dovre Wudali is a writer and editor from Saint Paul. She grew up on the plains of southwest Minnesota, where the wind blows strong and box elder bugs rule the earth. Her work has been published in *Creative Nonfiction*, *Sweet*, and *The Madras Mag* and is forthcoming in the *St. Paul Almanac*.

EDITORS

Laura Vosika

Laura Vosika is the author of *The Blue Bells Chronicles,* a tale of time travel, action and adventure, romance and redemption, across modern and medieval Scotland. She has had poetry published in *The Moccasin* and *Martin Lake Journal*. Her first collection of music has been released under the name *Glenmirril Garden.* She co-hosts *Books and Brews with Laura Vosika and Michael Agnew*, which features local authors and poets. Laura has been featured in newspapers, and on radio and TV.

Laura is the mother of nine and currently lives in Minnesota where she likes to attend open mics to read or play music.

Michael Dean

Michael Dean is the founder of and host of The Martin Lake Poetry Workshop and founder of and consulting editor for The Martin Lake Journal. His first poetry collection, *Sea Shells,* was published by Distillate Press, 2016. His poetry celebrates and memorializes his lifelong contact with Japan, Minnesota, and nature. He resides in the woods with his family and flat coat retriever near Martin Lake, Minnesota.

AFTERWARD

We hope you have enjoyed *Startled by JOY* and found some moments of joy within these pages!

At Gabriel's Horn, we offer a paying market to quality poets. The *Startled by* series will be an annual publication, released in May of each year. We invite you to submit to our upcoming volumes:

2020   Nature

2021   Love

2022   Laughter

2023   Music

2024   Faith

2025   Children

2026   America

2027   Legend and Lore

These are subject to change, particularly if we receive enough submissions to put out two anthologies per year. Our most current information: www.gabrielshornpress.com/poetry-anthology or contact gabrielshornpress@gmail.com

INDEX

Absher, J.S.

    Swallowtails on the Sandbar, 12
    Winter Beeches, 13

Anderson, Jacqueline

    The Bridge, 16
    Rockport, 16

Beck, Donna Marie

    Heliotropical, 11
    Ride, Charlie, 35

Blum, Dan

    On a Bicycle, 26
    Poem of Plight, 45

Bollman, J.M.

    Dance, 52-53

Burleson, Teresa

    The Transformer, 65

Centineo, Lorri

    A Few Eights on My Plate, 48
    Softer Rain, 62
    Summer Moon, 10

Connor, Mark

    My Now Departed Brother, 56-58
    Upon the Finishing of my House Fried Rice, 60-61

Felio, Deb

    In the Faces, 6

Gelle, Lilly

    Mystic Rose, 63
    Untitled, 64

Heathcote, Mark Andrew

    Joy, 8
    Joy Jumps Heart to Heart, 66
    I Should Like, 67

Hines, Mary Beth

    Honeymoon, 25
    December Song, 27

Hoffman, Robert Henry

    I saw my boy this morning..., 21

Hope, Rebecca

    On Making Snow Angels with My Son, 34
    He Gets the Credit, 47
    Confessions of a Non-Foodie, 46

Isaac, Donna

    August Morning, 55
    Making Do, 59

Meek, Ed
    Pinch Me Ghazal, 22

Moore, Annette
    Dance in the Rain, 11
    Morning Coffee, 29
    Slippy Sun, 29

Norman, Carter
    Come Remember, 32-33
    Echoes of the Morn, 36-37
    Ode to Yeats, 40-41
    All We Knew, 42
    Sweet Virgin of the Sacred Door, 68-69

Payne, Marc T.
    Haiku 1 on Family, 20
    Haiku 2 on Family, 20

Plocido, Tony
    Troublemaker, 30

Reid, Chris
    On Kianna Turning Two, 38-39

Reyes, Luisa Kay
    Flows Out Like a Stream, 7

Schneider, Kim
    Propitiation, 54

Sellers, J.A.

    Sea Song, 31
    New Joy, 50
    Still the Birds Sang, 51

Smith, Thomas R.

    Say Something, 14
    Mullein, Late July, 23
    Oak Leaf, 24
    You Know How, 24
    Simmer, 28
    Writing a Sonnet, 44

Swanson, Suzanne

    The Late Sonatas, Beethoven, Winter Sunday, 23

Tekkan

    Portrait, 15
    Golden Bumble Bees, 70

Vlooswyk, Mary

    Ebullient Bubbles, 17

Wudali, Sara Dovre

    My Stone Cat, 30

www.ingramcontent.com/pod-product-compliance
Lightning Source LLC
Chambersburg PA
CBHW031655040426
42453CB00006B/314